*A book
is a present you can open
again and again.*

THIS BOOK BELONGS TO

Andrew Silagi

FROM

Outside my Window

Written by Bernice Rappoport

Illustrated by Pamela G. Johnson

World Book, Inc.
a Scott Fetzer company
Chicago London Sydney Toronto

Copyright © 1992
World Book, Inc.
525 West Monroe Street
Chicago, Illinois 60661

Printed in the United States of America
ISBN 0-7166-1611-4
Library of Congress Catalog Card No. 91-65493

8 9 10 11 12 13 14 15 99 98 97 96

Cover design by Rosa Cabrera

Outside my window, who's in the grass?
Who's on the leaves and under the ground?
Who flutters about or maybe just crawls? Tiny
creatures, that's who! Come, step outside. Let's
take a peek.

Look up and down and all around.
Watch for things creeping and crawling,
flying and jumping, buzzing and hopping,
or just being still.

Sometimes we'll come close and see
what they are doing. Shhh . . . . Let's be
careful so we don't scare them away.

Here are some green caterpillars. Maybe
they stopped for lunch. What do you think they
are eating?

Small insects like these are sometimes hard to see. The color of their bodies matches the color of the things around them. That makes it easy to hide.

In a few weeks the caterpillars will look very different. They will change into something that might surprise you. Take a guess.

What did you guess would happen to the caterpillars? For about two weeks, they eat and eat until they get larger. Then they are ready to rest and to change into something called a pupa.

They cover themselves with a blanketlike wrap. A thin thread holds the changing creatures to a branch.While they rest, their bodies keep growing and changing.

In a few weeks the wrapping breaks open. Something pushes itself out. It is a creature with wings— a beautiful butterfly.

Butterflies flutter about on a sunny day like this. Some rest on bushes or on tree branches. Where has this butterfly stopped?

A butterfly has special mouthparts that work like drinking straws. It reaches into the flower center to sip the sweet juice, called nectar, from the flowers.

Did you know that butterflies help flowers grow? While they sip nectar, a powder from the flower, called pollen, sticks to the butterfly's mouth and legs. The butterfly drops some of this pollen in another flower. If the two flowers are the same kind, new seeds will begin to grow.

Honey bees like the sweet nectar from flowers, too. They store the juice in their bodies, in a little sack called a honey stomach.

The honey bees you see flying about might be carrying pollen, like the butterflies do. Honey bees save some of their pollen for a special recipe.

First they mix the pollen with nectar and make sticky lumps. Then they press the sticky lumps onto their back legs. Suppose we could follow the honey bees back home and see what they do with their "honey baskets" . . .

If we could see the inside of a beehive, it might look like this. Honey bees store the nectar in little cubbyholes called cells. As the water in it dries out, the nectar becomes honey.

Then the honey is food for the bees—but also for people. Some people know how to gather honey from a hive. They wear special clothing to protect themselves from the bees' stingers. The next time you eat honey, think about the busy bees.

And a beehive *is* a busy place. Some bees keep the hive clean. Others care for the babies. Another bee guards the door to keep other insects and animals away from the hive.

Here are some more curious little insects. Come up close to see the ladybugs. Their shells are like pretty, dotted coats.

Ladybugs keep their wings tucked under the shell. When they get ready to fly, the shell opens up to let the wings out.

Ladybugs don't search for nectar. Instead, they eat other small bugs, such as aphids. Some farmers collect ladybugs to keep other bugs from eating their fruit and vegetable plants. Do you think ladybugs might be called gardeners' friends, too?

What next? Ants, of course. These ants march along like hikers on a trail. The first ant has found something to eat. How do other ants know where to find the food? The first one leaves a special smell for them to follow.

Strong ants carry food back to their home. Ants might be living in the ground. If you could see the inside of their home, here is what it might look like.

The ants gather food and take care of the babies. They all work at building, repairing, and cleaning their home.

Ants are not the only busy workers under the ground. See the earthworms? They burrow through the soil, eating pieces of old plants that have fallen there. The worms keep the soil loose, and they mix in tiny pieces of old leaves that fall down as they wiggle along.

Hop! Jump! Who's that hopping in the grass? Now we know how grasshoppers got their name.

Grasshoppers are bigger than ladybugs and
ants, but they still need to be careful . . .

See how this one jumps right into trouble? The unlucky grasshopper is caught in a spider's web.

Spiders are another tiny creature you may see. To make their strong webs, they use a thin thread that comes from their own bodies. The spiders attach the thread to branches or other things.

A web can be as small as a penny or as large as a bedsheet. Spiders use their webs as traps to catch insects for food.

It's getting darker now. The curious insects and other creatures have worked hard all day. They tuck themselves under leaves or under a branch or in their homes. The night creatures will be out soon.

Listen, here they come. "Chir-r-rup" . . . "Chir-r-rup." It's the crickets. Crickets scrape their legs against their wings, back and forth, back and forth. That's how they make their sounds as they call out to each other.

The moths are out there, too. Moths are attracted by the glow of street lamps. They flutter about, looking like their butterfly cousins.

Crickets chirp, moths flutter, and what do fireflies do? They glow, that's what they do. Fireflies make a summer evening sparkle with a soft light their bodies give off.

The night is full of tiny creatures. Step back inside and you can still see them and hear them, outside your window.

Step Outside

Take a walk with your fingers. Follow the path.

Stop each time you see this sign **STOP**

Find the insect or other creature that belongs in each place.

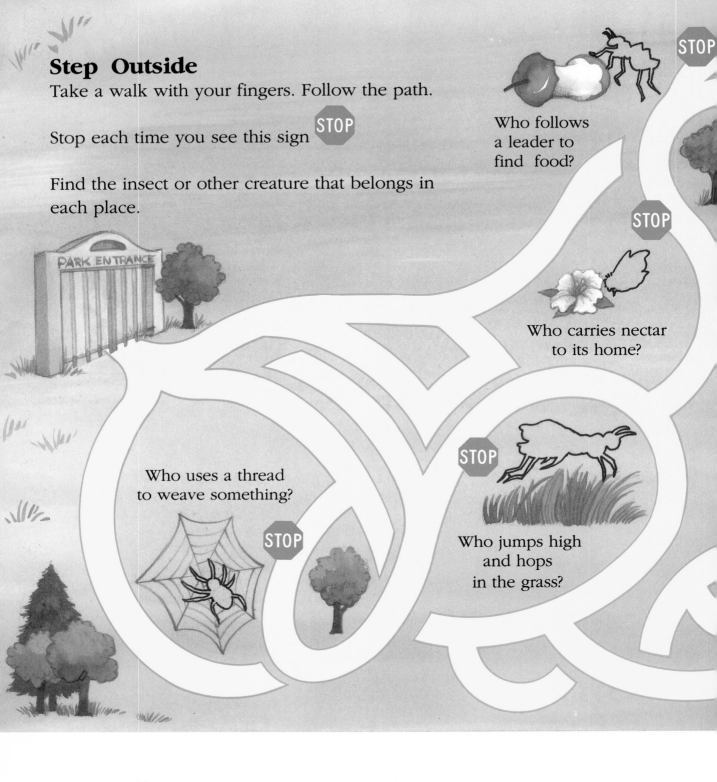

Who follows a leader to find food?

Who carries nectar to its home?

Who uses a thread to weave something?

Who jumps high and hops in the grass?

PARK ENTRANCE

Ladybug

Ant

Spider

Grasshopper

Who has round spots on its back?

Who flies around street lamps?

Who has a mouth like a drinking straw?

Who carries around its own light?

Who is a noisemaker at night?

PARK EXIT

Cricket

Firefly

Moth

Honey Bee

Butterfly

More About Curious Creatures

The curious creatures in this book are all insects except for spiders and earthworms.

Insects have these things in common:
- six legs
- a body with three sections—head, thorax, and abdomen
- two eyes—called compound eyes, because each has many tiny eyes

Most insects have two feelers, called antennae, on their heads. These help them touch and smell.

Spiders have eight legs and two body parts: a head and an abdomen. Most spiders have eight eyes.

Worms have no legs or backbones. Earthworms are one of several segmented types of worms.

How Insects Develop: The process of insects developing into adults is called metamorphosis. Depending on their special group, insects develop in one of these ways:

1. Eggs hatch into wormlike larvae that grow and shed their skin several times. Each one then transforms into a stage called the pupa. The pupa is often covered by a protective case called the cocoon. A butterfly becomes a chrysalis in its pupal stage. After a time, the adult pushes its way out.
2. The egg hatches and a tiny wingless copy of the parents comes out. The baby insects are called nymphs. They grow to become adults with full wings.

How Creatures Protect Themselves: Many insects and spiders are the same color as things around them. This is called protective coloration. Their bodies may be as green as grass, brown as tree bark, and so on.

Some insects and spiders use stingers or other mouthparts to injure their enemies. Others give off a bad smell that keeps enemies away. For example, the monarch butterfly tastes so bad that other creatures don't want to eat it.

To Parents

Children delight in hearing and reading about insects and other small creatures. *Curious Creatures Outside My Window* will provide your child with interesting information about a number of these, as well as a bridge into learning some important concepts. Here are a few easy and natural ways your child can express feelings and understandings about the insects and other small creatures in the book. You know your child and can best judge which ideas he or she will enjoy most.

When walking with your child, point out any small creature you may see. Say the name of the creature and ask your child to tell about it. For example, does the creature crawl? does it fly? or does it walk as we do?

Have fun singing "The Itsy Bitsy Spider" to your child, and do the hand motions that go with the song. Encourage your child to imitate the hand motions and to sing with you. Add a second verse about the "middle-size" spider, and then a third verse about the "great big" spider going up the water spout.

Play a special "creature" version of "Simon Says" with your child. For some of the "Simon Says" directions, ask your child to wiggle like a worm, hop like a grasshopper, buzz like a bee, and flap arms like a butterfly's wings. Think of some more animal movements that your child will have fun imitating. Imitate some of them yourself — your child will love watching.

Enjoy playing a game of "What Am I?" with your child. Think of an animal and then give clues about what the animal is. For example, say, "I was once a caterpillar. I crawled across a leaf. I don't crawl anymore. Now I fly. What am I?" Keep giving clues until your child names the creature.

On your next walk, encourage your child to pretend to be a scientist who wants to learn about ants. Take along some drawing paper and crayons or a notebook and pencil. Encourage your child to describe what the ants you find are doing. Write down the description. Your child may want to draw a picture of the ants at work.

Your child can make a glittering spider web. With glue or a glue stick, have your child draw a spider web on a piece of paper. Let your child sprinkle glitter onto the web to make it sparkle. When the glue is dry, your child might want to draw a spider.